Laura Ingalls Wilder

Read These Other Ferguson Career Biographies

FERGUSON
CAREER BIOGRAPHIES

Laura Ingalls Wilder

Teacher and Writer

BY LUCIA RAATMA

Ferguson Publishing Company
Chicago, Illinois

Photographs ©: Bettmann/Corbis, cover; Laura Ingalls Wilder Home Association, 8, 12, 15, 21, 26, 58, 62, 74, 78, 81, 95, 97; Hoover Library, 10, 25, 38, 44, 53, 66, 77, 86, 90, 92; North Wind Picture Archives, 17, 49, 69; Corbis, 22, 29, 33, 35, 40, 82; Archive Photos, 46, 100.

An Editorial Directions Book

Library of Congress Cataloging-in-Publication Data
Raatma, Lucia.
    Laura Ingalls Wilder : teacher and writer / Lucia Raatma.
    p. cm. — (Ferguson career biographies)
    Includes bibliographical references and index.
    ISBN 0-89434-375-0
    1.Wilder, Laura Ingalls, 1867–1957—Juvenile literature. 2. Authors, American—20th century—Biography—Juvenile literature. 3. Frontier and pioneer life—United States—Juvenile literature. 4. Children's stories—Authorship—Juvenile literature. [1. Wilder, Laura Ingalls, 1867–1957. 2. Authors, American. 3. Women—Biography. 4. Frontier and pioneer life.] I. Series.
PS3545.I342 Z82 2001
813'.52—dc21
[B]   00-049044

Copyright © 2001 by Ferguson Publishing Company
Published and distributed by
Ferguson Publishing Company
200 West Jackson Boulevard, Suite 700
Chicago, Illinois 60606
www.fergpubco.com

Printed in the United States of America
Y-3

CONTENTS

Laura Ingalls Wilder

In 1900. Laura Ingalls Wilder pauses at a spring near her home in Mansfield, Missouri.

A STORY TO TELL

Laura Ingalls Wilder lived during a very exciting time in United States history. When she was a child, America was growing. More and more people were moving west into the territories. These areas weren't even called states yet. Laura and her family were pioneers, some of the first white people to live in these territories.

Laura grew up in many places because her family moved many times. Laura's life was filled with adventure and sometimes danger. She worked hard and spent lots of time outdoors. When Laura was older, she

Inside the farmhouse. Laura Ingalls Wilder wrote her Little House series while living here.

wanted to remember the early days of her life. So she began to write about them.

The stories she told were made into books. And children from all backgrounds loved reading about Laura's homes and friends and family. Her books became famous, and Laura became one of the most beloved writers in the United States.

One of the most amazing things about Laura Ingalls Wilder's career was when it started. She did not become a published writer until she was forty-four years old. And she did not publish her first book until she was sixty-five. But she had been preparing to be a writer for years and years. She lived in many homes and had all kinds of experiences. She always enjoyed reading and telling stories. So by the time Laura and her husband were settled at Rocky Ridge Farm in the Ozark Mountains, she had much to say.

In a letter to some fans, she explained her writing and her life this way:

The Little House books are stories of long ago. The way we live and your schools are much different now; so many changes have made living and learning easier. But the real things haven't changed. It is still best to be honest and truthful; to make the most of what we have; to be happy with simple pleasures and to be cheerful and have courage when things go wrong.

The Ingalls girls. Carrie, Mary, and Laura (left to right) pose for a picture in the 1880s.

PIONEER GIRL

Laura Ingalls was born on February 7, 1867, in an area known as the Big Woods. This land was near Pepin, Wisconsin. It was full of forests and wild animals. At that time in Wisconsin, towns were very small and were far away from one another.

Laura's sister Mary was two years old when Laura was born. Their parents were Charles and Caroline Ingalls. Both Charles and Caroline came from families who were Wisconsin pioneers.

Close Families

Charles was originally from New York state, but his family settled near Concord, Wisconsin, when he was a young boy. He had eight brothers and sisters. All the brothers grew up working on farms. They learned to hunt and trap wild animals. They went to school only when they were not needed to work. Even so, Charles loved reading, and he enjoyed school whenever he could go.

The Ingalls family also enjoyed having fun. Charles learned to play the fiddle and often played for neighborhood dances. Among the Ingallses neighbors were the Quiners. This family also came from the eastern United States.

Caroline was the Quiners' oldest child. She came from a big family too. Even as a child, she was quiet and serious. She liked to write poetry and she loved to read. When Caroline grew up, she became a teacher. She taught for two school terms and earned $3 a week. Caroline and Charles Ingalls often met at church and at dances. Soon they began spending more time together.

In 1860, Charles and Caroline got married. Theirs was not the only marriage between the Ingallses and the Quiners though. Caroline's brother

Devoted parents and pioneers. Charles and Caroline Ingalls made a home for their family no matter where they lived.

Henry married Charles's sister Polly. And Caroline's sister Eliza married Charles's brother Peter.

Starting a Family

Shortly after their marriage, Charles and Caroline Ingalls moved to the Big Woods of Wisconsin. It was there that they started their family. Their first child, Mary Amelia, was born on January 10, 1865. Laura Elizabeth was born two years later.

Laura remembered little things about her early years in the Big Woods. She remembered how strong her father was. And she remembered her mother singing her to sleep. Uncle Henry and Aunt Polly had moved nearby, so the two families spent much time together.

But it wasn't long before the Ingallses left their cozy house in the Big Woods. Charles longed for the open prairie. He wanted to own a large piece of land and farm its rich soil.

The Homestead Act

In 1862, President Abraham Lincoln signed a law called the Homestead Act. This law gave U.S. citizens a chance to own public land for free. Much of the land west of the Mississippi River had not yet

Homesteaders in the 1860s. The Homestead Law gave many people the chance to own land in the American West.

been settled. Portions of this land had been divided into 160-acre (65-hectare) squares. Any U.S. citizen over the age of twenty-one could claim one of these pieces of land and be a homesteader. There were a few rules however. A house had to be built on the land. The land had to be lived on for at least six months of the year. And the land had to be farmed. Then, after five years, the homesteader became the official owner of the land.

This was a wonderful opportunity for many people. They were excited by the idea of open prairie. The idea of owning a farm was appealing to many families who lived in cities and other crowded places. Charles Ingalls was one person who couldn't wait to move farther west.

To Kansas

When Laura was only two years old, the Ingallses sold their farm to Gustaf Gustafson. Mr. Gustafson was a Swedish immigrant who had come to Wisconsin with his family. The Ingallses loaded their belongings into a covered wagon and began the very long trip to the prairies of Kansas. Pa and Ma, as Laura called her parents, knew it would be a big adventure. But they felt it was the best move for their family. After traveling for many weeks, they settled in an area near the brand-new town of Independence, Kansas.

There Pa built a house made of logs. The floor was made of dirt, and their front door was only a quilt at first. Laura and Mary helped unpack all of their belongings. They remembered to bring Pa's fiddle and all of Ma's books. Soon the four walls became a home for the Ingalls family.

Laura came to love Kansas. She enjoyed the sun on her face and running through the tall grasses. Mary was much more ladylike, however. She never took off her bonnet in the sun. Instead she liked to stay inside and sew.

Mary and Laura were different in many ways. Mary had beautiful blond hair and blue eyes. Laura had brown hair. Sometimes Laura was jealous of the way her sister looked. Also, Mary was quiet and serious, while Laura was full of energy. Nevertheless, the two girls were constant companions as they grew up. And they came to love each other very much.

While the girls played together and helped Ma in the house, Pa stayed busy working the land. He plowed the fields and dug a well. He built a barn and helped nearby farmers as well.

Native American Territory

As the Ingalls family settled into their new home, there was one problem. They learned that they had moved onto land that was not meant for homesteaders. The land in fact belonged to a group of Native Americans called the Osage people. The Osage had been away hunting when the Ingalls family arrived.

At first the Osage were very friendly. They would see Pa in the woods when he was hunting. Sometimes they visited the Ingallses at their cabin. Ma shared food with them and was kind to them. Laura liked listening to them talk in their strange language. And she liked to look at the beads and feathers they wore.

A New Sister

While the family was in Kansas, another daughter was born. Laura and Mary's new sister was named Caroline Celestia, but everyone called her Carrie. She was born on August 3, 1870.

Leaving Their Land

More and more settlers continued to come to the Kansas prairies. And as they came, rumors spread that the Native Americans were becoming angry. Some people believed there would be a war over the land. At night, the Ingallses could hear the Indians chanting. Laura remembered, "It was far more terrifying a sound than the howling of wolves."

Pa began to fear for his family. He was not sure what the Osage would do. In the meantime, the U.S. government suggested a solution. Congress offered

The third sister, Carrie Ingalls was born in August 1870.

the Native Americans money for their land. Congress also offered the tribe a new reservation in another state. The Osage accepted the offer and soon left to live on a reservation.

Sadly, the fate of the Osage was not uncommon in the American West. Many Native Americans had their land taken from them. Some went to war and fought for their homeland. But many were forced to leave their land and travel to reservations far from their homes.

Forced from their land. Members of the Osage tribe lost their land when white settlers moved west.

Back to the Big Woods

Shortly after the Osage left, the Ingallses received a letter from Mr. Gustafson, who had bought their farm. He could no longer pay for it, and he wanted them to take the farm back. Pa and Ma Ingalls talked about what to do. Ma hated to leave the home they had made in Kansas. But she was also eager to see her brothers and sisters.

So in 1871, the family loaded their wagon once again. They headed back to the Big Woods with their dog, Jack, trotting along behind them.

Back in Wisconsin, aunts and uncles and cousins surrounded Mary, Laura, and Carrie. It was a fun time for the family. They gathered together for big meals, and they listened to Pa Ingalls play the fiddle at night.

That spring, Mary started attending the Barry Corner School, which was not too far from the farm. She and her cousins walked there each day. Laura, who stayed home with Carrie, felt terribly left behind, and she was eager to start school herself. But for several months, all she could do was wait for Mary to return every afternoon. Every day, Mary showed Laura her books and told her all that she had learned each day.

The next fall, Laura began school as well. She

loved reading and writing. And she enjoyed being around all the other children.

When the weather was bad during the winter, Mary and Laura had to stay home from school. Then Ma helped them keep up with their lessons. And she also taught them to cook and sew.

For two years, the Ingallses did well in the Big Woods. Pa worked hard, and the farm produced good crops of wheat. But, as more people settled around them, Pa longed for open space. He remembered the prairies of Kansas, and he began to talk of moving west again.

In the Wagon Once Again

Although Ma loved Wisconsin, she knew how much her husband wanted to move on. They talked to Uncle Peter and Aunt Eliza, who also wanted to move. Soon the two families agreed to go to Minnesota. They had to leave in the winter before the ice on Lake Pepin began to melt. They actually traveled in their wagons across the frozen lake!

After they all reached Minnesota, Uncle Peter found a farm to settle. But Pa wanted to go to the western part of the state. So Laura and her family continued on without her aunt, uncle, and cousins.

Charles Ingalls. Pa worked hard to provide for his wife and children.

They spent many weeks on the trail, and they watched winter turn to spring. Wildflowers bloomed, and the grass turned green. Birds flew overhead and called to one another against a bright blue sky. At night, Ma cooked over a campfire, while Pa played the fiddle. Laura loved these days and remembered them her whole life.

A young woman. As she grew older, Laura Ingalls came to understand her father's desire to be a pioneer.

TO WALNUT GROVE AND BACK

After a long trip on the dusty trail, the Ingalls family finally reached the small town of Walnut Grove. It was in the southwestern part of Minnesota. Near Walnut Grove was a lovely spot called Plum Creek. It was there that Pa bought 172 acres (70 ha) of land.

An unusual house was already on the farm. It was a dugout—a house built into the earth. It was only about the size of their wagon, and grass grew on its roof. It looked something like a cave.

Level prairie land lay all around the dugout. Pa was eager to plant and harvest wheat. He had finally found the wide-open space he had been looking for.

Life on Plum Creek

The dugout was small, but it quickly became a home for the Ingallses. Everyone slept on straw-filled mattresses, and Ma cooked on a small stove. Mary and Laura had chores to do each day. They helped make the beds, and they carried fresh water from the creek. They both worked on their sewing too. Mary enjoyed this work, and her stitches were always quite neat. But Laura hated to be inside. She wanted to be out in the fresh air and sunshine.

So the two sisters also made time to play. They enjoyed exploring the creek and gathering flowers. They picked plums and chased butterflies over the prairie grasses. They played with Carrie and their dog, Jack, as much as they could. Meanwhile, Pa plowed the prairie. He was preparing the land for a wheat crop that he was sure would make them rich.

Off to School

Before long, Mary and Laura started going to school in Walnut Grove. Many other families had moved to

Part of the earth. The Ingallses lived in a dugout home that looked something like this.

the small town, so there were lots of other children there as well. At first, Laura was afraid to meet all these new people. But she and Mary soon came to like the school. Both girls were good students. And Laura especially liked playing with the other children at recess.

The only children she didn't like were Nellie and Willie Owens. Their parents owned the general store in town. Nellie and Willie thought they were better than all the homesteading children, and they could be very mean. Years later when she wrote about them, Laura changed their names from Owens to

Oleson. She didn't want to use their real names, because they had always been such difficult people.

Building a Church

Walnut Grove was growing so much that the people soon needed a church. Pa and Ma helped to organize the Union Congregational Church in town. The minister sent to run the church was Reverend Edward Alden. He soon became a good friend to the Ingalls family. He called the sisters his "country girls."

In December 1874, when Laura was almost eight, the new church was ready. The town had a special party just before Christmas to celebrate. Laura couldn't believe how beautiful the Christmas tree was. It was the first one she had ever seen! And everyone was given presents donated from churches back east. Laura received a jewel box as well as a fur muff and cape. It was a happy time for Walnut Grove.

A Minnesota Winter

In the next few months, the Ingallses learned what blizzards were like. That winter was cold and dangerous. Winds blew and many, many feet of snow fell. People could easily get lost in a blizzard because the snow and sleet made it impossible to see. Even cattle sometimes wandered off and would be found miles away. Blizzards could last for several days.

Laura later wrote, "The blizzards always came quick enough to catch people unprepared. No one measured the speed of wind in those days, but it surely was as fast as hurricane speed. Whichever way one went into the blizzard, he went against it."

A Promise of Good Times Ahead

The long, snowy winter meant more moisture in the ground. Many people believed it would mean better crops the following summer. So Pa was sure that the wheat he had planted would be a plentiful crop. In fact, he was so sure that he decided to build his family a new house.

He bought all the materials on credit, promising to pay when his crop was harvested. Everyone in town believed in the crops too, so they were happy to give Pa what he needed. He bought lumber and windows and doors.

Each day, Mary and Laura watched their new house being built. A neighbor helped Pa build the frame of the house. They nailed shingles on the roof, and they installed the windows. The sisters couldn't believe how beautiful the finished home was.

When they moved in, Mary and Laura shared the attic. Ma got a new stove downstairs. Sunshine seemed to stream through every window. Outside, the wheat was growing tall and green; it would soon be ready for harvest. The whole family was excited about their new home and what the future would bring.

Grasshoppers!

But one day, the family's dreams came to a frightening end. The sky grew dark as though a big storm was coming. However, clouds did not cause the darkness. It was a huge swarm of grasshoppers making its way across the prairie.

The insects landed in the fields and began eating everything in sight. They devoured the trees, the flowers, and the vegetable gardens. Worst of all, they ate the wheat crops. By the time they laid their eggs and flew away, the wheat fields were destroyed. All that the Ingallses and so many other families had worked for was gone.

Laura later remembered, "I have lived among uncounted millions of grasshoppers. I saw their bodies choke Plum Creek. I saw them destroy every green thing on the face of the earth."

The dark sky. Swarms of grasshoppers destroyed wheat fields throughout Minnesota.

Many families gave up and went back east. Stores shut down and schools closed. It was as though the grasshoppers took all the life from Walnut Grove.

Laura wondered if her family would have to move out as well. But, after all their work, Ma and Pa decided they could not leave their farm. Instead, Pa decided to find work harvesting other people's crops.

He needed the money to pay for the many things he had bought on credit. The grasshoppers had destroyed all the nearby crops, so he had to travel farther away. He walked for more than 200 miles (322 kilometers) to eastern Minnesota before he found work.

While he was gone, Laura and Mary helped Ma work on the farm. But they all missed Pa terribly. So they were very happy when he returned home with the money that they all needed.

Another Try

The Ingallses had decided to stay in Walnut Grove for another season. They hoped that the next crop would be better.

In the fall of 1875, Ma gave birth to another child. This time it was a boy, named Charles Frederick. The girls started calling their little brother Freddie, and they loved playing with him.

The next spring Pa planted wheat, and soon it began to grow. But as the weather warmed up, the eggs laid by the grasshoppers began to hatch. The young grasshoppers grew and soon devoured the wheat just like their parents had.

A healthy crop. The Ingallses longed for fields of wheat to harvest, but the grasshoppers ended their dream two years in a row.

Pa and Ma began to give up. They didn't see how they could go on living in Walnut Grove. Soon, they loaded the covered wagon once again. Pa was very disappointed. His dreams of the West had not worked out. The family traveled east to live with Uncle Peter and Aunt Eliza on their farm.

Moving On

The move to Uncle Peter and Aunt Eliza's was a temporary one. Pa had been offered a job in Burr Oak, Iowa. He and Ma were asked to take care of a hotel there. So Laura and her family stayed with their relatives just for that summer.

Pa helped with Uncle Peter's harvest and all the cousins enjoyed playing together. But it was not a happy time.

Freddie had been sick soon after he was born. He grew more ill on the trip and was terribly weak. Ma and Pa had a doctor come to see him, but nothing helped. Then, in August, Freddie died. It was a sad day when the family buried him near Uncle Peter's farm. He was only nine months old.

Before long, it was time to go to Burr Oak. The family loaded up the wagon again. And they said good-bye to Freddie's grave.

Living in Burr Oak

The Ingallses tried to adjust to Burr Oak, but they found it hard. The town was older and noisier than anywhere they had lived before. The hotel they managed was called the Burr Oak House. The family lived in the hotel along with the guests.

Laura Ingalls Wilder: Teacher and Writer

Mary and Laura helped out by washing dishes and by making beds. They waited tables and cared for the younger children. But even with the girls' help, Ma had so much to do. She did the laundry as well as the cooking and cleaning. It was also a difficult time for her. She was sad about losing Freddie. But she was also expecting another child. This made her happy in many ways, but it also made her very tired.

Another problem was the saloon next door to the hotel. The customers were noisy, and they often drank too much. Ma felt that this was no place for her girls to be growing up. She voiced her concerns to Pa, and soon the family went to live above a grocery store in town. Later, they moved to a brick house outside of town.

Mary, Laura, and Carrie all went to school in Burr Oak. Laura continued to enjoy reading and writing, but she never liked math. She also liked reading aloud, and she worked on her speaking skills.

In May 1877, another little sister was born. Her name was Grace Pearl. Laura thought the new baby was beautiful. And the whole family hoped that she was the beginning of better times for everyone.

Another sister. Grace Pearl was born in May 1877.

A Strange Offer

One day Ma Ingalls received a strange offer from Mrs. Starr, one of the most important women in Burr Oak. Mrs. Starr and her husband had a big house and were quite rich. Their daughters were grown up and no longer lived at home. Mrs. Starr told Ma how lonely the big house was and how fond she was of Laura. She suggested that the Ingallses give Laura to the Starrs. She and her husband would raise her as their daughter and, Laura would have fine clothes and a good education.

Laura listened to this conversation from another room. She was frightened by the idea of being given away. She couldn't imagine living without Pa and Ma and her sisters. So she was terribly relieved when Ma turned down the offer. Mrs. Starr went home to her big house alone.

Leaving Burr Oak

The Ingallses lived in Burr Oak for just over a year, but they never felt quite suited to the town. Pa still wanted land of his own. And Laura remembered loving the wide-open spaces of the West. It was time to move on.

The family packed their wagon once again and headed back to Minnesota. They were returning to Walnut Grove! The trip was a happy one. Pa played his fiddle each night by the campfire, and everyone looked forward to what lay ahead. They missed Freddie, but they felt lucky to have baby Grace. And when they arrived in Walnut Grove, it was as though they had never been away. Laura later said, "Burr Oak seemed like a dream from which we had awakened."

Minnesota marketplace. The Ingallses bought supplies and sold goods in stores like this one.

GROWING UP 4

When the Ingallses returned to Walnut Grove, they didn't live on a farm as before. At first, they lived with another family, the Ensigns, while Pa built them a new house. He worked in a local store and did carpentry jobs for people throughout town. Later on, he opened up a butcher store. He was a good businessman, and he did well for his family.

Settling In

When the family moved into their new home, they enjoyed each other's company.

The Ensigns had been very kind to them, but the Ingallses were so happy to be on their own. Pa was relieved to be away from the noise of Burr Oak. Ma enjoyed activities at church, and she was very happy to be settled once again. At night, Pa would play his fiddle, and Mary and Laura learned to dance to his tunes.

Mary, Laura, and Carrie went to school in Walnut Grove with many of the children they had known before. Nellie Owens was still mean. But she had a new rival—Genevieve Masters, the daughter of the schoolteacher. Laura just kept her distance from both of them. She liked being a tomboy. And she joined many of the boys at school in playing baseball and handball.

On Her Own

One summer Laura was offered a job at the local hotel. She washed dishes, made beds, and helped clean up. And sometimes she took care of the hotel owner's little boy. She earned 50 cents a week. And when things were quiet, she would sit down with copies of the *New York Ledger* that belonged to the owner. Laura loved reading stories about people from faraway places.

Soon other people in town noticed what a hard worker Laura was. She began running errands and taking care of children for lots of families. She was happy to help. Money was tight in the Ingalls household, and Laura liked being able to help out.

Becoming Mary's Eyes

Suddenly, in the winter of 1879, Mary became very sick. Her head and throat hurt, and she had a high fever. A doctor said that she had "brain fever," which probably meant meningitis—an infection in the brain. For weeks, Mary lay in bed, and then her eyesight began to fail. The doctor said her nerves had been damaged. Before long, Mary was completely blind.

Laura couldn't believe that her beautiful sister could no longer see. But Pa gave Laura an important job. He told her that she was to be Mary's "eyes" from then on. She was to describe everything to Mary—the colors, the lights, everything that was going on in the world. It was an important task for twelve-year-old Laura.

The whole time she had been sick, Mary had never complained. And even after going blind, she never said an angry word. Laura was impressed by

Mary in the 1880s. Laura's older sister lost her eyesight and relied on Laura to describe everything for her.

her sister's strength. She tried to help out around the house as much as she could.

More Changes

Ma and Pa had begun to worry about money again. They had doctors' bills to pay. And they weren't making enough money from the store and Pa's other odd jobs.

At that time in the United States, the railroad was becoming a big business. Railroad tracks were being built farther west. Soon, trains were carrying supplies and settlers into the new territory. Pa was once again longing to go west, but he didn't have the money to do it.

One day, however, he got an exciting offer. His sister Docia came to Walnut Grove for a visit. Her husband, Hiram Forbes, was helping to build the railroads. They asked Pa if he would like to manage a store for the railroad company in the Dakota Territory. This area later became North and South Dakota.

Pa was thrilled. The pay was good, and he would be moving west. There was still land to homestead in the Dakota Territory too. But Ma worried about moving again. She didn't know how Mary would get

Crossing the country. The railroads changed the American West because traveling and sending supplies became easier.

along in such wild country. But Pa promised that if they moved this time, they would never move again, so Ma agreed. The railroad company needed Pa right away, so he planned to leave with Aunt Docia. The rest of the family would follow later. The night before Pa left, the family dog died in his sleep. Poor Jack had followed the Ingallses on all their travels, but he couldn't manage another trip. The family buried him along one of his favorite paths in Walnut Grove.

After a few months, Pa sent money for Ma and the girls to join him. The packed up their belongings and prepared to leave Walnut Grove once again. When the big day came, they boarded a train for the very first time, and their trip into the Dakota Territory began. Laura remembered, "The engine's round front window glared in the sunshine like a huge eye. The smokestack flared upward to a wide top, and black smoke rolled up from it. A sudden streak of white shot up through the smoke, and the whistle screamed a long wild scream."

The train was an exciting experience. Laura described the windows and the seats to Mary. She told her all about the sights they passed and the people around them.

Pa met Ma and the girls at the end of the railroad. At that time, the tracks went only so far into the Dakota Territory. There the family lived in a railroad camp along with the men who were building the railroad. As more tracks were laid, the crew and the Ingallses moved along as well. Each time, they packed their things and moved a little farther west. Finally, they settled on the edge of Silver Lake.

Making a Home in De Smet

The town that grew along Silver Lake came to be called De Smet. It was named for Father Pierre Jean De Smet, a Catholic priest from Belgium. He served as a missionary in the Dakota Territory.

During the first winter in De Smet, the Ingallses lived in a house that belonged to the railroad. The railroad workers had gone back east until spring so Pa was asked to stay and take care of the house. The family had a good winter there. There was plenty of space and lots of food, and they were protected from the cold and snow. Pa hunted in the nearby woods and searched for a homestead for the family. Finally, he settled on 160 acres (65 ha) about 1 mile (1.6 km) from town.

As the months went by, the Ingallses often had visitors. The railroad house was the only building for miles around, so people often asked to stay the night. Sometimes Ma felt as though they were running a hotel again, but she enjoyed the company.

One welcome visitor was Reverend Alden. He was traveling throughout the west and helping to start new churches. During his visit, he held a church service right in the house for the Ingallses and another family. Ma realized with pride that it

Father Pierre Jean De Smet. The town of De Smet was named for this Catholic missionary.

was the first church meeting in the new town of De Smet. Also, Reverend Alden spoke to the Ingallses about a school for the blind in Vinton, Iowa. He knew it was a good school, and he thought Mary would enjoy going there. It was then that Laura began to think about her future as well.

De Smet's First Teacher

Laura knew that the family would need money to send Mary to the school in Iowa. She also knew that Mary had always wanted to be a teacher. And Ma, once a teacher herself, had looked forward to seeing the teaching tradition continue. Originally, Laura had never considered being a teacher. She loved the outdoors and hated being cooped up inside. But she was a good student, and she loved books. So very soon, she began to make plans for her own teaching career.

After their first winter in the Dakota Territory, the family moved briefly into town. Pa had bought some land in De Smet and had started constructing some buildings there. At first, Laura hated living in the partially completed house on Main Street, but then she decided to make the best of it. She started an informal school for Carrie and her friends. She told herself that if she was going to be a teacher, she should start early and learn to be a good one. She was only thirteen at the time.

Back on the Prairie

As soon as they could, the Ingallses moved from town out to the homestead land. Pa had built a shack there and it soon became a home for them. Laura helped Ma in the house and the garden. She also helped Pa clear the fields and plant trees.

When there was time, Laura took Mary for long walks. She described the sunsets and the flowers. She told her sister about the trees and the birds. Mary once said, "You make pictures when you talk, Laura." Such words were quite a compliment. No wonder Laura would one day write wonderful stories about her life.

As the summer ended, a new school was started in De Smet. Laura and Carrie attended, while Mary stayed home with Ma. At night, Laura read her lessons to Mary, and the girls studied together.

A Hard Winter

As the fall of 1880 turned into winter, it became terribly cold. The Ingallses returned to Main Street to live. Being closer to other people seemed safer during the bad weather. Blizzards hit the area over and over again. By this time, about eighty people lived in De Smet. They ran a few businesses, and they all relied on the railroad for supplies.

But when the weather grew more dangerous, the trains stopped coming. Snowdrifts covered the tracks. The school closed, along with many of the businesses. Almanzo and Royal Wilder owned the grain and feed store in town. The brothers supplied the people of De Smet with hay and flour. Then supplies began running low. People began to worry about having nothing to eat. They were afraid to leave their homes even between blizzards, never knowing when another one would start.

During this time, Almanzo Wilder made a daring trip. He and Cap Garland, one of Laura's schoolmates, crossed the prairie in search of wheat. They had heard of a settler with a large supply. They found the man, bought some wheat, and hauled it back to town. They returned just as another blizzard hit. The two young men no doubt saved the people of De Smet from starvation.

In April, the storms finally ended, and the ground began to thaw. The following month, the first train got through to De Smet. The long, hard winter was over.

Sending Mary to School

That summer, the Ingallses moved back to their homesteaded land, and Laura got a job in a De Smet store. Mary was going away to the Iowa school in the

Young Almanzo Wilder. The Ingallses were impressed with his efforts to help the people of De Smet during a long, hard winter.

fall, and Laura wanted to help out. She saved the money she made—$9 by the end of the summer—and gave most of it to Ma and Pa for Mary's expenses.

The family missed Mary when she left for school, but everyone was excited for her too. In addition to her regular studies at the school, Mary learned to play the piano and organ. And she learned more about sewing. She mastered fancy stitches and beautiful beadwork. She even learned to make hammocks.

Teacher in Training

During the next two winters, the Ingalls family moved back to the house in town. Laura liked being near the school. She was concerned about her education because she wanted to earn her teaching certificate. She had to be sixteen to do that.

At that time, teaching school was much different from how it is today. Schools were often one-room buildings. Classes were very small and frequently made up of children of all ages. And teachers were not trained in college and graduate school as they are today. They just had to pass a test in order to teach.

Laura became friends with many of her classmates. But she was very disappointed when Genevieve Masters arrived at school one day. She and her family had also moved to De Smet. Genevieve was still as mean as she had been in Walnut Grove. Laura tried to ignore her, but it was difficult in such a small town.

The schoolteacher in De Smet was Eliza Jane Wilder, Almanzo's sister. She was a bright young woman but she could not control the children in the classroom. Laura felt that she was not learning all that she could. So she was relieved when Miss Wilder stopped teaching. Other teachers followed, and Laura was determined to study hard. She wanted to be ready to teach.

In Front of the Class

The opportunity came to Laura more quickly than she had ever expected. Shortly after performing at a school recital in December 1882, she was approached by Robert and Ellie Boast. The Boasts had visited the Ingallses when they lived in the railroad house. The Boasts and their cousin, Mr. Bouchie, were very impressed with Laura. Mr. Bouchie ran a school 12 miles (19 km) south of De Smet, and he wanted Laura to teach there.

Laura couldn't believe it. She was still a few months shy of her sixteenth birthday. Mr. Bouchie told her not to worry about her age. He arranged for her to meet with the school superintendent, who was also quite impressed with the young woman. By the end of the day, Laura had her teaching certificate!

She was hired by Mr. Bouchie to teach for January and February. And she would earn $20 a month. The money would definitely help with Mary's school costs.

Unfortunately, the setup for teaching at the Bouchie School was rather hard. Laura had to live with Mr. and Mrs. Bouchie and their young son. Mrs. Bouchie was never kind to Laura, so Laura hated living in their house. She was very homesick and wanted so much to go to De Smet each weekend. But traveling 12 miles (19 km) in the winter was difficult, so she didn't mention the idea to Pa.

However, much to her surprise, someone came to bring her home at the end of her first week. It was Almanzo Wilder, sitting on a sleigh behind a team of Morgan horses. It was a terribly cold winter, but every Friday, Almanzo came to get her. And every Sunday, he took her back. Laura was shy around the young man, and often they barely spoke on their trips back and forth.

Back to School

When her first teaching job was over, Laura returned to school in De Smet. Professor Owen was the instructor, and he encouraged Laura in all her studies. He especially stressed her writing. For years Laura had written poetry and rhymes, but Professor Owen told her to write more about the things around her and about the books she had read.

Laura appreciated all of the teacher's advice. She worked hard and tried to set a good example for the younger students.

Making Time for Romance

When Laura had finished her term at the Bouchie School, she politely told Almanzo that she did not wish to ride with him anymore. She did not know how he felt about her. But she was secretly interested in Cap Garland.

Nevertheless, Almanzo hoped Laura would change her mind. So very often, he appeared at the Ingalls home with his sleigh and invited Laura out. Soon she began to reconsider the young man. He was kind, and she enjoyed his attention. And Pa had always had great respect for Almanzo.

*Bessie and Manly. After taking time to get to know one another,
Laura and Almanzo were married in 1885.*

On their trips in Almanzo's sleigh, and later in his buggy, they talked about all kinds of things. Laura learned that he loved horses and that he was ten years older than she was. As they grew closer, they made up nicknames for one another. Laura called him "Manly." And Almanzo—after discovering Laura's middle name, Elizabeth—began calling her "Bessie." It wasn't long before the two of them were inseparable.

A Teacher Once Again

In the spring of 1884, Laura began her second position as a teacher. She taught for the months of April, May, and June at the Perry School. The school was only a short walk from the land the Ingallses were homesteading. Laura enjoyed this job much more than her first one. She had only three students, and she was paid $25 a month.

As she taught, she also continued to study. Her own education was not yet over, and Laura still had much she wished to learn.

Plans for the Future

Over the summer, Laura and Almanzo spent much time together. They went to church and celebrated the Fourth of July. They rode horses and went to dances. The months were filled with joy and hope.

Then one night, Almanzo asked Laura to marry him. She was seventeen, and he was twenty-seven. He felt they were old enough to plan their own futures. Laura agreed, and she happily accepted a gold engagement ring set with pearls and garnets. Pa was pleased with the news, and Ma said with a smile, "Pa and I haven't been blind. We've been expecting it." Laura and Almanzo decided to marry the following year.

In the fall of 1884, Laura began her last year of high school. Professor Owen was still the instructor, and the school was now a two-story building. But, as odd as it may sound, Laura did not finish her final year. She decided that she wanted to teach school for one more term. And since married women were not allowed to teach at that time, she wouldn't have too many more chances. Professor Owen was very sad to see her go.

In the spring of 1885, Laura taught at the Wilkins School. The school was several miles north of De Smet, which meant that she again had to live away from home. But the Wilkins family she stayed with was very kind to her. Laura enjoyed the position, and she earned $30 a month. She was not homesick this time, but she loved spending time with her fiancé. So, just as before, Manly picked her up every weekend.

That summer, Mary visited, and the sisters spent many hours together. They took long walks and talked about Mary's school. Times were changing. And by their next visit, Laura would be a married woman.

At age twenty-five. By this time, Laura was married, had become a mother, and had lived through some difficult times.

MARRIAGE AND MOTHERHOOD

Laura and Almanzo knew what kind of wedding they wanted. So when they learned that Almanzo's sister Eliza Jane wanted to plan a big ceremony for them, they decided to act more quickly. On August 25, 1885, they had a simple service at the local minister's house. Then they drove to the Ingalls home for dinner.

After that, they traveled a few miles away to the house Almanzo had built for them. It was a quiet, wonderful day. And by the end of it, Laura Ingalls Wilder was thrilled to realize, "I had a house and a home of my own."

Making a Home

The land the Wilders owned was quite generous. Almanzo had made two homestead claims instead of just one. The extra one was a tree claim. This was allowed because he agreed to plant young trees there. But it meant that the young couple lived on more than 300 acres (122 ha) of land.

Though they both knew what a risky business it could be, Laura and Almanzo decided to try farming. Laura had learned a great deal from her father as she was growing up, and she felt she could now help her husband.

Running a farm was very expensive, especially at first. Many supplies were needed, including plows and other machinery. Laura helped out a great deal, and the couple managed to save money by not hiring outside workers. Their bills were growing, but they were convinced that their first crop of wheat would solve all their problems.

Laura worked on the house too. She tried hard to make it a home as Ma had always done for her family. She cooked and sewed, and she kept the rooms tidy. Very soon, Laura discovered she was expecting a baby. The future held much promise.

Difficult Times

One August day, not long before the wheat was due to be harvested, a storm blew across the prairie. Huge pieces of hail beat down on the ground. The storm did not last long, but the damage was terrible. The wheat crop was completely destroyed. No doubt, Laura had memories of grasshoppers as she gazed at the ruined fields.

Laura and Almanzo had no choice but to try again the following year. In the meantime, though, they had bills to pay. They decided to rent out their home and land for a while. During that time, they lived in the little house Almanzo had occupied before their marriage. It was not an ideal situation, but it was the best they could do.

A New Baby

While they were living in the smaller house, the young couple's baby was born. In early December, Laura went into labor. Ma and a neighbor were at her side and helped her through the many difficult hours. And finally, on December 5, Laura gave birth to a little girl. She was named Rose after the flowers that bloomed in the fields each year.

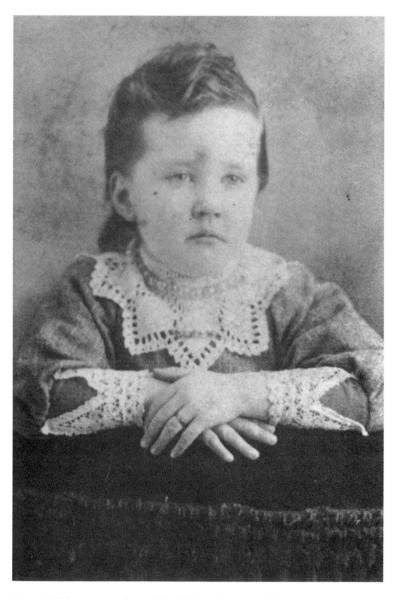

Rose Wilder at age four. The Wilders' only child was born on December 5, 1886.

In the months that followed, Laura stayed close to home. She took care of the house and her new baby. Almanzo worked on the farm, preparing to plant a new crop of wheat.

As the weather warmed up, Laura began helping on the farm again. She kept Rose nearby in a basket as she worked in the fields. One day, a black St. Bernard dog appeared at the Wilders' door. He seemed to like Rose, so the family took the dog in. He became Laura's helper in watching the baby.

More Troubles

Laura and Almanzo had hoped that the next crop of wheat would end their money worries. But they had very little rain that year, so the harvest was small. Laura later wrote of "how heartbreaking it was to watch the grain we had sown with such high hopes wither and turn yellow in the hot winds!" Almanzo was certain they could be successful farmers if they were patient and worked hard. But so far, their luck had not been good.

Meanwhile, Laura's parents had given up their homestead. They moved into town, and Pa worked as a carpenter. Carrie and Grace were still in school, so the family enjoyed living in De Smet again. Laura often brought Rose by for visits.

In the winter of 1888, Rose stayed with her grandparents during a very difficult time. Both Laura and Almanzo contracted diphtheria. This disease can cause an infection in the heart and nervous system. Almanzo's brother Royal stayed in the house to help out, and Laura and Almanzo slowly got better. But the disease left them both weak. Almanzo was especially affected. His legs were partially paralyzed, and he had difficulty walking.

After that illness, Almanzo found it even harder to take care of the farm. There were many tasks he simply could not do. Laura helped as much as she could, but they could not work all the land. So they sold half of their acres and moved back into their original home. Also, with the help of Laura's cousin Peter, the Wilders began raising sheep. Given the unpredictable weather, they felt they could not rely only on growing wheat.

The next season was as dry as the last, and the Wilders had another bad year. But they looked forward to new life, as Laura was expecting another child. One hot day in August, she gave birth to a little boy. Everyone was excited by his arrival but,

A sheep ranch. The Wilders began raising a herd like this one in hopes of making extra money.

sadly, the baby did not live. He was buried in the De Smet cemetery, and he remained without a name.

Laura was overwhelmed by grief. She didn't talk to anyone about the little boy. All she wanted was rest and quiet.

Shortly after the baby died, there was an accident in the kitchen. Laura was feeding the stove fire, and perhaps one of the burning sticks was dropped. The whole kitchen quickly went up in flames. Laura managed to get herself and Rose out of the house, but there was nothing she could do about the fire.

She screamed for help, but the house burned to the ground. Only a few things, such as some silver and china, were saved.

Laura felt as though they had lost everything. Farming had not worked. They owed money to many people. Sickness had made both of them weaker. And they had lost an infant son. It was hard to decide what to do next.

On the Road

Before long, Laura and Almanzo decided to visit his parents in Spring Valley, Minnesota. They sold their sheep and gave half of the money to cousin Peter. Then they packed the few things they had, said good-bye to the Ingallses, and headed east.

Laura enjoyed the time in Minnesota. She loved getting to know her in-laws and the relatives appreciated meeting little Rose. She was a favorite with all the family and friends.

The Wilders stayed in Minnesota for more than a year. And then they decided to try Florida. Someone suggested that the warm weather might be good for Almanzo's health. So this time, they headed south.

It turned out that Florida was not the place for

them, however. Laura felt out of place there, and some people even called her a "Yankee woman," referring to her northern background. She found the weather humid and uncomfortable. They left in less than a year.

At this point, Laura and Almanzo decided to go home. Soon they were on their way to South Dakota. In 1889, the Dakota Territory had become the states of North and South Dakota. The Ingallses were thrilled to have Laura and her family living just a block away in De Smet.

Laura began working in a dress shop, while Almanzo did carpentry and other odd jobs. During the day, Rose enjoyed staying with her grandmother and Aunt Mary. They taught her to knit and to sew.

But Laura and Almanzo still dreamed of having their own piece of land. They had given up on wheat but not on farming altogether. They wished for a smaller farm. And they considered a milder climate for Almanzo. People had told them about land in the Ozark Mountains in Missouri. There the hills were lush and green. Orchards were plentiful and produced apples and other fruits. Soon they decided to give the Ozarks a try.

To Rocky Ridge Farm

On their last night in South Dakota, the Wilders had dinner at the Ingalls home. Laura enjoyed being surrounded by Ma and Pa, Mary, Carrie, and Grace. She looked at their faces and wondered when she would see them again. After dinner, they all sat together on the porch and listened to Pa play his fiddle. It was a wonderful, yet sad evening for everyone.

The next day, Laura, Almanzo, and Rose got into their covered wagon and began their journey. Laura had saved $100 from her job at the dress shop, and she hid the money away, knowing it would buy land for their new home. Laura also decided to keep a diary on the trip. She thought it would be interesting to keep a record of her thoughts and of all that happened along the way. Her first entry was labeled "July 17, 1894."

The Wilders spent nearly a month and a half traveling in the covered wagon. Sometimes the weather was terribly hot and the days seemed endless. Rose complained and cried. She missed Aunt Mary and the others.

To comfort her daughter, Laura often held her close and told her stories. She told her about times when she was a girl. She told her about adventures with Aunt Mary, Aunt Carrie, and Aunt Grace. Rose loved hearing the stories and begged to hear them again and again.

Each night, as they camped along the trail, Laura wrote in her diary. She told Rose "It is like a letter to myself." She also wrote letters home and told her family about everything they saw on their journey.

Finally, after traveling all the way through Nebraska and Kansas, the Wilders entered Missouri. The land became more hilly and green. Laura felt a cool breeze and she noticed the large shady trees. They reminded her of the Big Woods of Wisconsin. In a letter to Pa, Laura said of the Ozarks, "They are beautiful. We passed along the foot of some hills and could look up their sides. The trees and rocks are lovely. Manly says we could almost live on the looks of them."

Soon the family arrived in Mansfield. As the wagon pulled into town, Laura announced, "This is where we stop." They looked around the village and saw pretty houses with shade trees. They saw a two-story schoolhouse and a train depot. And around the little town were acres of green farmland and orchards. Laura wrote in her diary, "There is everything here already that one could want."

Mansfield Town Square in 1900. The Wilders knew they had found a wonderful place to live when they arrived here in 1894.

The Wilders camped in the woods for a few weeks as they looked for a farm to buy. And soon they found just what they were looking for. It was 40 acres (16 ha) about 1 mile (1.6 km) or so from Mansfield. The land was rocky and rough, which made Almanzo worry. But Laura knew the place was perfect. They used Laura's $100 as a down payment and Laura named their new home Rocky Ridge Farm.

Home at Last

Rocky Ridge Farm came with a small log cabin and 400 young apple trees ready to be planted. Laura began making the small cabin into a home. And Almanzo began clearing the land for farming. The wood he cut down was used for fuel during their first winter.

Almanzo was still not as strong as he had once been so he often needed Laura's help. She learned to use a saw, and the two of them cut down trees. With the wood, they built fences and a henhouse. And they sold the remaining wood in town. With much hard work, they managed to turn their land into a fruit, dairy, and poultry farm.

In the spring, they planted the apple trees and a vegetable garden. The apple trees would take years to produce a real crop so, in the meantime, the Wilders sold eggs from their chickens and milk from their cow. Almanzo also bought a prize-winning Morgan horse and decided to become a breeder.

Between the apple trees, they planted strawberries and raspberries. Laura also made butter and sold it in town. And she increased the size of the chicken flock. Their little farm was prospering, and finally the Wilders felt at home.

Watching Rose Grow Up

While Laura and Almanzo had been tending to their new farm, their daughter was growing up. She was a very smart girl, and she had quickly become bored in school. Laura encouraged her to read and to borrow books from the library. So Rose read poetry and books about history and romance. She developed very strong opinions and sometimes even argued with her teachers. The people of Mansfield weren't quite sure what to make of this young woman.

Laura sympathized with her daughter. She remembered what it was like to be the smartest in the class. And she remembered sometimes feeling as though she didn't fit in.

When Rose was finishing her last year of school in Mansfield, Almanzo's sister made an interesting offer. She had moved to Crowley, Louisiana, and she wanted Rose to come live with her. There, Rose could graduate from high school. This was something she could not do in Mansfield, where the school only went as far as the eighth grade.

Laura and Almanzo considered what was best for Rose, and soon they agreed to the plan. For a year, Rose lived in Louisiana and studied all kinds of subjects. She even learned the equivalent of four years

All grown up. The Wilders were proud to hang Rose's graduation portrait in their home at Rocky Ridge Farm.

of Latin in that period of time. And in the spring of 1904, she graduated at the top of her class.

When Rose returned to Mansfield, her parents proudly hung her graduation picture on their wall. But they knew that Rose could not be happy in the Ozarks. She did not enjoy life on a farm, and she longed for adventure. Laura advised Rose to learn to send telegrams by working a telegraph. People used telegrams to communicate quickly in those days before telephones and electronic mail had been invented. This skill would help Rose get a good job. But Laura knew that such a job would be far away from Mansfield.

At age thirty-nine. Laura Ingalls Wilder's life became more and more interesting as she grew older.

A WRITING LIFE

6

As Laura had predicted, Rose moved away. She went to Kansas City and was soon hired by Western Union. Then she moved on to San Francisco. There she married Claire Gillette Lane, a newspaper reporter. Rose's life was exciting, and she had lots of dreams.

With their daughter grown up and out of the house, Laura and Almanzo put all their efforts into farming. They designed and built a frame house near the log cabin they had been living in. Each year, they added on and made the house larger. When it was finished, it had ten rooms, four porches, a large kitchen, and a library. After so many years of living in cramped cabins, Laura loved all that space.

Over the years, Laura also worked hard on the farm. She took very good care of her flock of chickens. And soon everyone in the Ozarks knew what a successful poultry farmer she was. Her knowledge of farming led to a new career for her.

Newspaper Writer

When Laura was forty-four years old, John Case, an editor for the *Missouri Ruralist* newspaper, asked her to send him some articles for publication. Laura was thrilled by the idea. She began to write many pieces about farming and life on Rocky Ridge Farm. She wrote about making a small farm work, and she wrote about women's roles on the farm. She had one column entitled "The Farm Home" and another called "As a Farm Woman Thinks." Her byline was "Mrs. A. J. Wilder."

Laura went on to sell her articles to other newspapers as well. She had pieces published in the *St. Louis Post-Dispatch* and the *Kansas City Star*. Many of her readers agreed that Mrs. A. J. Wilder "knows farm folks and their problems."

A young career woman. Rose Wilder Lane became an accomplished journalist and wrote about many important people.

San Francisco in 1905. Laura enjoyed visiting her daughter in this busy and exciting city.

Mother and Daughter

Rose had traveled a great deal during her first years of marriage. She visited Rocky Ridge Farm when she could, but she was very busy. At one point, she gave birth to a baby boy. But sadly, just as in her mother's case, the baby did not live. Rose came to the farm after this loss and was happy to recover with her parents close by.

Aside from that tragedy, however, Rose was living a full life. She was enjoying herself in San Francisco and had become an important writer. She worked for the *San Francico Bulletin*. First she wrote love stories, but then she moved up to write feature articles. She interviewed many famous people including car manufacturer Henry Ford and actor Charlie Chaplin.

When Laura asked Rose for advice on her farming articles, Rose was eager to help. But she wanted to do so in person. She begged Laura to come to San Francisco for a visit. "I simply can't stand being so homesick for you anymore." Laura left the farm in her husband's hands and made plans to travel west.

San Francisco

When Laura arrived in San Francisco in 1915, the city was holding the Panama-Pacific International Exposition. This fair celebrated the city's recovery from the terrible earthquake of 1906. It also celebrated the newly opened Panama Canal. The canal would make the city's ports busier and improve trade. Laura and Rose had a wonderful time at the fair. There was so much to see—gardens and art shows, rides and games, and so many, many people. Laura sent articles about it to the *Missouri Ruralist* for publication.

The city was exciting for Laura, but she missed Mansfield during her four months away. She wrote many postcards to Almanzo and described all the sights. Rose wanted her parents to move to California, but neither of them wanted to leave Missouri. As Laura said in a letter to her husband, "I love the city of San Francisco. It is beautiful but I would not give one Ozark hill for all the rest of the states that I have seen."

Separate Lives

Once back in Missouri, Laura resumed all her work around the farm. She continued writing her articles. And she joined the Mansfield Farm Loan Association. Mansfield was a growing community. So Laura and Almanzo spent much time entertaining and getting to know their neighbors.

Beyond the house they were so proud of, the Wilders tended their plentiful orchards. They grew apples, pears, and peaches as well as strawberries and raspberries. These fruits were sold in Mansfield or shipped to St. Louis and Memphis. They also raised cows and sold a variety of dairy products.

In the meantime, Rose saw the world. She had been divorced in 1918, so she spent all her time writing. She traveled to New York and all over Europe. She wrote biographies of Henry Ford, Jack London, and Herbert Hoover. She wrote *Diverging Roads*, a novel about a woman struggling with her marriage and career. Her book *Peaks of Shala* was about a dangerous trip she made in Albania. She dedicated that book to her mother. Rose also published stories in *Harper's*, *Good Housekeeping*, and other magazines. People all over the country were beginning to know the name Rose Wilder Lane.

Rose worried about her parents, however. She didn't want them to work so hard, and she wished she could make enough money to let them retire. Until that happened, she was very generous. In 1925, she gave Laura and Almanzo their first car. It was a Buick that they named Isabelle. Both Laura and Almanzo learned to drive it. But Laura preferred horses, so her husband did most of the driving.

At one point, Rose also had a new house built for their parents. It was an English cottage made of stone. Its features were very modern, quite unlike the farmhouse they were used to. And its furniture came from a fancy department store. The Wilders lived in the cottage for a time, but eventually moved back to the farmhouse they had built themselves.

Rocky Ridge Farm. The Wilders were proud of their farmhouse and the surrounding property.

Loss and Change

Rose often wrote letters to her mother and Laura enjoyed sharing these with family and friends. Laura also wrote many letters to her sisters and tried to keep up with her family. But the Ingalls family was changing.

Pa had died in 1902, and Laura had traveled back to De Smet to be at his side. Years later, in 1924, Ma died, and Mary went to live with Carrie and her husband. A few years after that, Mary died too. Laura began to think more and more about her family, and she wanted to find a way to remember them. She wanted to write down all of Pa's stories, and she wanted to tell about her life on the pioneer trail.

One day—at the age of sixty-three—she sat down with a tablet and began writing. For several months, she wrote. She told about her family's move to Kansas and then back to the Big Woods. She told about Plum Creek and Burr Oak. She told about De Smet and teaching and falling in love with Almanzo. When she was finished, she titled the story "Pioneer Girl."

Publishing Her First Book

Laura showed her written pages to Rose and asked for her help. Rose typed the pages for her and suggested many changes. First, they shortened the story and called it "When Gramma Was a Little Girl." They submitted the story to an agent named George Bye, but he turned it down.

Then Rose suggested that Laura make the story mostly about her life in Wisconsin. And she thought the book should be written for older readers. Laura followed her daughter's advice, and the story was sent to George Bye again. Laura didn't really expect to publish a book, but she loved reliving her childhood days.

Much to her surprise, Laura received a telegram on Thanksgiving Day. It was from an editor at Harper and Brothers, a publisher in New York. They wanted to publish Laura's story. The book was retitled *Little House in the Big Woods*, and it was published in April 1932. Laura was sixty-five years old.

Always a Writer

What Laura may not have realized was that she had been preparing to be a writer all her life. As a child, she loved reading and listening to stories. In school, she enjoyed writing poetry and rhymes. Later, she used words and her visual skills to describe the world to her sister Mary.

On her trip to Missouri, she kept a diary, and she told stories to Rose to keep her entertained. And most of all, Laura followed a rule that many writers follow. She wrote about things she knew. First she wrote about farming, and then she wrote about her life. The stories she told were a part of her, and who better to tell them!

Success and Fame

Little House in the Big Woods was very successful, and it was named a Newbery Honor Book. This meant it was runner-up to the Newbery Award Book, the best children's book of the year. Soon Laura began getting mail from her readers.

The editors at Harper and Brothers were so pleased that they asked Laura to write another book. So she wrote *Farmer Boy*, a story about Almanzo and his childhood in New York state. It was published in 1933.

As Laura received more letters from children, she realized that she had many stories to tell. So next, she wrote about life in Kansas. This book, *Little House on the Prairie*, was published in 1935. Following that, she wrote about Minnesota. *On the Banks of Plum Creek* was published in 1937 and was named a Newbery Honor Book.

Revisiting the Past

Laura was enjoying her life as a writer. The people of Mansfield appreciated her fame, but Laura tried to live a normal life. She still worked on the farm and cooked meals for Almanzo. To her, she was still the same person she had always been.

Before she wrote her next book, she decided to revisit her home in De Smet. Laura and Almanzo traveled north to South Dakota, where they arrived

Back to De Smet. Almanzo and Laura returned to South Dakota to celebrate Old Settler's Day in 1939.

just in time for Old Settler's Day. They were able to see many of their old friends. And they had great fun seeing how much things had changed. Laura also got to spend time with her sisters Carrie and Grace.

Following her trip, Laura wrote her next book about life in De Smet. She titled it *By the Shores of Sil-*

ver Lake, and it was published in 1939. This book also won a Newbery Honor.

The next year, *The Long Winter* was published. It told about the hard winter of 1880–1881. Then she wrote *Little Town on the Prairie* and *These Happy Golden Years.* The last book ended with her marriage to Almanzo. It was published in 1943 when Laura was seventy-six.

Sharing Stories with the World

In the years that followed, Laura's words reached readers all over the world. Her books were published in many languages. They were even published in Braille, the "language" used by blind readers. Laura continued to receive mail from thousands of children. She got requests for autographs and pictures. Teachers sent her questions, and some children even sent her drawings. She loved the letters she found in her mailbox every day. And she insisted on answering every single one.

In her seventies. Laura Ingalls Wilder was a famous writer as she neared the end of her life.

STORY'S END 7

As the Little House books continued to sell, Laura suddenly had more money than ever before. She no longer had to rely on income from the farm. Her royalty checks allowed the Wilders to live a comfortable life.

Laura and Almanzo still enjoyed their time at Rocky Ridge Farm and within the Mansfield community. They attended church each Sunday and took long drives in the Ozarks.

Honors and Awards

In 1948, Laura received wonderful news. The Detroit Public Library planned to open a new branch. And they wanted to open it in the name of Laura Ingalls Wilder. It marked the first time that a U.S. library was named for a woman and for a living person. Laura was very honored, but she felt she was too old to attend the ceremony. Instead she sent the original drafts of *The Long Winter* and *These Happy Golden Years*, along with a special letter.

Also the children's department in a library in Pomona, California, was named for her. Laura sent that library the original draft of *Little Town on the Prairie*.

In 1951, Mansfield also named their library for their famous resident. She attended that ceremony and was overwhelmed by the attention. School-children sang to her, and a local band played. It was a wonderful day.

Harper and Brothers decided to continue their success with Laura's books. In 1953, the publisher released new editions of all the titles. Garth Williams illustrated these editions. Before drawing his pictures, Garth Williams had visited the sites of all of Laura's homes and had come to know the areas. He

Many years together. Almanzo and Laura both lived to be in their nineties.

met with Laura, and she told him lots of stories. His illustrations captured the spirit of Laura's life, and she was delighted with them.

The next year, the American Library Association created an award in her name. The Laura Ingalls Wilder Award honors authors or illustrators who make lasting contributions to children's literature. Laura received the first medal, which was designed by Garth Williams. The award continues to be given today.

Endings

Amid all the honors and all the excitement, however, Laura experienced sad times too. Carrie died in 1946, and Laura mourned the loss of her sister. Then in the summer of 1949, Almanzo had a heart attack. He was left very weak, and Laura had to help him each day. As the weeks passed, he seemed to be getting better. But then, on October 23, he suddenly died.

Laura did her best to go on without him but she missed him terribly. The ten-room house seemed too big without him. They had been married for sixty-four years.

Meeting her readers. Laura enjoyed visiting bookstores and signing books for her fans.

Her agent George Bly—and her readers—had been asking her to write more. Laura had been working on "First Three Years and a Year of Grace," which was about her early married years. But after her husband died, she put the story away. Without Almanzo by her side, she couldn't bear to write about the difficult years they had survived together.

Almanzo had lived to be ninety-two, and Laura thought that was something to be proud of. She decided that she also wanted to live to the age of ninety. In her later years, she remained as active as she could. She spent time with neighbors, and she enjoyed seeing Rose when she was able to visit. But by the fall of 1956, Laura's heart was weak and she had diabetes.

Laura stayed close to home that winter, and Rose came to be with her. On February 7, 1957, Laura turned ninety. She opened cards from friends and fans, and she appreciated all that life had given her. Three days later she died.

Stories that Live On

After her death, Laura was buried in the Mansfield cemetery next to her husband. Readers around the world were sad to know she was gone. But her stories live on to this day.

While Rose was packing up things in the Rocky Ridge house, she discovered her mother's diary. This was the journal she had kept during their trip from South Dakota to Missouri. Rose read the entries and knew they were special, so she typed them up and added her own memories, creating *On the Way Home*. This book was published in 1962.

Years later, Laura's stories became the basis for a television series. During the 1970s and 1980s, *Little House on the Prairie* was a popular program starring Melissa Gilbert as Laura and Michael Landon as Pa. People of all ages enjoyed watching the Ingalls family week after week.

Today, the Little House books are still favorites at the library and the bookstore. New generations of readers continue to discover the work of Laura Ingalls Wilder. They love to read about journeys and troubles, about growing up and growing old, and about families and the love that they share. Laura Ingalls Wilder was a wonderful storyteller, and as her sister Mary once told her, she made pictures when she talked.

The cast of Little House on the Prairie. *This television show was very popular in the 1970s and 1980s.*

TIMELINE

1867   Laura Ingalls born on February 7 in the Big Woods of Wisconsin

1869   Settles with her family near Independence, Kansas

1871   Travels back to the house in the Big Woods

1874   Moves to Plum Creek outside Walnut Grove, Minnesota

1876   Moves to eastern Minnesota; then moves to Burr Oak, Iowa

1877   Returns to Walnut Grove

1879   Moves to De Smet in what is now South Dakota

1880–1881   Survives a long and difficult winter

1882   Earns her teaching certificate

1883   Teaches at the Bouchie School

1884   Teaches at the Perry School

1885   Teaches at the Wilkins School; marries Almanzo Wilder on August 25

1886   Gives birth to a daughter, Rose, on December 5

1889	In August, gives birth to a son, who later dies before he is named
1894	Travels with Almanzo and Rose to Mansfield, Missouri; purchases Rocky Ridge Farm
1911	Becomes a published writer when her first article appears in the *Missouri Ruralist* farm journal
1932	Publishes her first book, *Little House in the Big Woods*
1933	Publishes *Farmer Boy*
1935	Publishes *Little House on the Prairie*
1937	Publishes *On the Banks of Plum Creek*
1939	Publishes *By the Shores of Silver Lake*
1940	Publishes *The Long Winter*
1941	Publishes *Little Town on the Prairie*
1943	Publishes *These Happy Golden Years*
1949	Almanzo dies on October 23
1953	New editions of all the Little House books are produced with new illustrations by Garth Williams
1954	The Laura Ingalls Wilder Award is created
1957	Dies on February 10 at Rocky Ridge Farm
1962	*On the Way Home* is published
1970s–1980s	*Little House on the Prairie* enjoys several seasons as a popular television show

HOW TO BECOME A TEACHER

The Job

Elementary-school teachers instruct pupils from the first through sixth grades. They develop teaching outlines and lesson plans, give lectures, organize discussions and activities, keep class-attendance records, assign homework, and evaluate student progress. They usually work with one group of pupils for the entire school day, teaching several subjects and supervising lunch and recess.

Most elementary-school teachers teach one grade. In some smaller schools, however, grades are combined. And there are still a few elementary schools in remote rural areas, where all eight grades are taught by one teacher.

As an elementary-school teacher, you'll teach language, science, mathematics, and social studies. In the classroom, various methods are used to educate students. You may read to them from a book, assign group projects, and show films. You'll teach them educational games and help them come up with ways to remember new information. Students in kindergarten and the first and second grades are taught the basic skills—reading, writing, counting, and telling time. Older students are taught history, geography, math, English, and handwriting.

Creating interesting exercises and activities takes time outside of the classroom. In addition to this extra work, you'll prepare daily lesson plans, including lists of student assignments. You'll also grade papers and tests, keep a record of each student's progress, and prepare reports for parents. You'll meet with teacher aides to discuss how they can help in the classroom. You'll keep the classroom orderly and neat and decorate the desks and bulletin boards.

Music, art, and physical education are usually taught by teachers who specialize in those areas. *Art teachers* develop art projects, gather supplies, and help students develop drawing, painting, sculpture, mural design, ceramics, and other artistic abilities. Some art teachers also teach the history of art and organize field trips to local museums. *Music teachers* teach music appreciation and history. They also direct student choruses, bands, or orchestras or simply accompany a classroom of students in singing. Music teachers are often responsible for organizing school pageants, musicals, and plays. *Physical-education teachers* help students develop coordination, strength, and stamina as well as social skills, such as self-confidence and good sportsmanship. Physical-education teachers often coach school sports teams and organize field days and community activities.

Elementary-school children are taught social skills along with general school subjects. The teacher helps the students learn right from wrong. He or she also maintains a system of rewards and punishments.

Recent developments in school programs have led to such concepts as the ungraded or multi-age classroom, where one or more teachers work with students within a small age range. Some schools are also turning to bilingual education in which students are instructed throughout the day in two languages, either by one bilingual teacher or two teachers who concentrate on different languages.

Requirements

High School Your school's college-preparatory program will offer advanced courses in English, mathematics, science, history, and government to prepare you for an education degree. Art, music, physical education, and extracurricular activities will give you the wide knowledge necessary to teach a variety of subjects. Composition, journalism, and communications classes will help you develop good writing and speaking skills.

Postsecondary About 500 teacher-education programs are offered in the United States. Most of these programs are designed to meet the requirements of the state in which they're located. Some states may require that you pass a test before being admitted to an education program. In most states, an elementary-education teacher must major in elementary education. Programs vary among colleges but may include introduction courses in the teaching of reading, guidance of the young child, children's literature, and teaching language arts. Practice teaching, also called student teaching, in an actual school situation is usually part of the program. The student is placed in a school to work with a full-time teacher. During this period, the student observes how lessons are presented and how the classroom is managed, learns how to keep records of attendance and grades, and gets actual experience in handling the class—both under supervision and alone. Some states require a master's degree; teachers with master's degrees can earn higher salaries. Private schools do not require an education degree.

Licensing and Certification   Public-school teachers must be licensed under regulations established by the Department of Education of the state in which they are teaching. Not all states require teachers in private or parochial schools to be licensed. When you've received your teaching degree, you may request that a transcript of your college record be sent to the licensure section of the state Department of Education. If you have met all the requirements, you will receive a certificate saying you are eligible to teach in the public schools of your state. In some states, you may have to take additional tests.

Other Requirements   The desire to teach is based on a love of children and a dedication to their welfare. You must respect children as individuals, with likes and dislikes, strengths and weaknesses of their own. You must be patient and self-disciplined and have a high standard of personal conduct. Teachers make a powerful impression on children, and you'll want to be a good role model.

Exploring

Volunteer to teach elementary classes in Sunday school or become an assistant in a scout troop. You might work as a counselor in a summer camp or assist a recreation director in a park or community center. Look for opportunities to tutor younger students or coach children's athletic teams. Your local community theater may need directors and assistants for summer children's productions. Many day-care centers hire high-school students for late-afternoon and weekend work. Working with preschoolers will give you a sense of a child's learning processes and the methods used to educate young children.

Employers

Elementary-school teachers are needed at public and private schools, parochial schools, Montessori schools, and day-care centers that offer full-day elementary programs. Although some rural areas have elementary schools, most are in towns and cities. Teachers are also finding opportunities in charter schools—smaller, deregulated schools that receive public funding.

Starting Out

After completing the teacher-certification process, including student teaching, your college's placement office will help you find full-time work. Also, the Departments of Education of some states provide listings of job openings. And many schools advertise teaching positions in the classified ads of major newspapers. You may also want to contact the principals and superintendents of schools in which you'd especially like to work. While waiting for full-time work, you can work as a substitute teacher. In urban areas with many schools, you may be able to substitute full-time.

Advancement

Most teachers become experts in the job they have chosen. Usually salaries increase as teachers gain experience. Additional training or study can also bring more money.

A few teachers may advance to the position of principal. Others may work up to supervisory positions, and some may become helping teachers. These teachers help other teachers to find appropriate instructional materials and develop their courses of study. Others may go into teacher education at a college or university. Additional education is required for most of these positions. Some teachers also become guidance counselors or resource-room teachers.

Work Environment

Usually, you'll work in a pleasant environment, although some older schools may have poor heating and electrical systems. The job of the elementary-school teacher is not strenuous, but it can be trying. You must stand for many hours each day, do a lot of talking, exhibit energy and enthusiasm, and handle any discipline problems. But problems with students are usually overshadowed by the successes. The work of an elementary teacher can be confining, because you are with your pupils constantly throughout the day's activities. School hours are generally 8:00 A.M. to 3:00 P.M., Monday through Friday. Teachers are usually able to take all school holidays, including winter and spring vacations. Many teachers take college courses during the summer months to help them do a better job. Some states require teachers to take such courses to renew or upgrade their teaching licenses.

Earnings

Most teachers are contracted to work nine months of the year, though some contracts are made for ten or twelve months. (When children are not present, teachers are expected to do summer teaching, planning, or other school-related work.)

The National Education Association's (NEA) *Rankings of the States, 1997,* reported the average annual teacher salary was $38,611, ranging from $26,764 in South Dakota to $50,647 in Alaska. The American Federation of Teachers also released survey results for 1997–98. Its report found that the average beginning salary for a teacher with a bachelor's degree was $25,700. The average maximum salary for a teacher with a master's degree was $44,694. Teachers can supplement their earnings through teaching summer classes, coaching sports, sponsoring a club, or other extracurricular work.

Teachers have unions that bargain with schools over wages, hours, and benefits. Most teachers join the American Federation of Teachers or the National Education Association (NEA). Depending on the state, benefits include a retirement plan, sick leave, and health and life insurance. Some systems grant teachers sabbatical leave.

Outlook

The U.S. Department of Education predicts that 1 million new teachers will be needed by the year 2008 to meet rising enrollment and replace retiring teachers. The NEA believes this will be a difficult challenge because of low teacher salaries. Higher salaries will be necessary to attract new teachers and keep experienced ones, along with other changes such as smaller classes and safer schools. Other challenges for the profession involve attracting more men. The percentage of male teachers continues to drop.

To improve education for all children, changes are being considered by some districts. Some private companies are now managing public schools. Although some believe that a private company can provide better facilities, faculty, and equipment, this has not been proved. Teacher organizations are concerned about taking school management away from communities and turning it over to corporations. Charter schools and voucher programs are two other controversial alternatives to traditional public education. Charter schools are small schools that are publicly funded but not guided by the rules and regulations of traditional public schools. They are viewed by some as places of innovation and improved educational methods, but others see charter schools as ill-equipped and unfairly funded with money that could be used to benefit local school districts. Vouchers, which exist in only a few cities, allow students to attend private schools by using public money for tuition. These vouchers are paid for with public tax dollars. In theory, the vouchers allow for more choices in education for poor and minority students, but private schools still have the option of being highly selective in their admissions.

TO LEARN MORE ABOUT TEACHERS

Books

Davidson, Margaret. *Helen Keller's Teacher*. New York: Scholastic, 1996.

McDaniel, Melissa. *W.E.B. Dubois: Scholar and Civil Rights Activist*. Danbury, Conn.: Franklin Watts, 1999.

Shephard, Marie Tennant. *Maria Montessori: Teacher of Teachers*. Minneapolis: Lerner, 1996.

Wilker, Josh. *Confucius: Philosopher and Teacher*. Danbury, Conn.: Franklin Watts, 1999.

Websites

American Federation of Teachers

http://www.aft.org

For more information about teaching from a professional union

National Education Association
http://www.nea.org
For more information about education and teaching

Where to Write
American Federation of Teachers
555 New Jersey Avenue, N.W.
Washington, DC 20001
202/879-4400
For information about teaching careers from their professional union

National Education Association
1201 16th Street, N.W.
Washington, DC 20036
202/833-4000
For information about careers and about the current issues affecting teachers

HOW TO BECOME A WRITER

The Job

Writers are involved with the expression, editing, promoting, and interpreting of ideas and facts. Their work appears in books, magazines, trade journals, newspapers, technical studies and reports, company newsletters, radio and television broadcasts, and even advertisements.

Writers develop ideas for plays, novels, poems, and other related works. They report, analyze, and interpret facts, events, and personalities. They also review art, music, drama, and other artistic presentations. Some writers persuade the general public to choose certain goods, services, and personalities.

Writers work in the field of communications. Specifically, they deal with the written word for the printed page, broadcast, computer screen, or live theater. Their work is as varied as the materials they produce: books, magazines, trade journals, newspapers, technical reports, company newsletters and other publications, advertisements, speeches, scripts for motion-picture and stage productions, and for radio and television broadcasts.

Prose writers for newspapers, magazines, and books do many similar tasks. Sometimes they come up with their own idea for an article or book, and sometimes they are assigned a topic by an editor. Then they gather as much information as possible about the subject through library research, interviews, the Internet, observation, and other methods. They make notes from which they gather material for their project. Once the material has been organized, they prepare a written outline. The process of developing a piece of writing involves detailed and solitary work, but it is exciting.

When they are working on an assignment, writers submit their outlines to an editor or other company representative for approval. Then they write a first draft of the manuscript, trying to put the material into words that will have the desired effect on their readers. They often rewrite or polish sections of the material, always searching for just the right way of getting the information across or expressing an idea or opinion. A manuscript may be reviewed, corrected, and revised numerous times before a final copy is submitted.

Writers for newspapers, magazines, or books often specialize in a specific subject. Some writers might have an educational background that allows them to give a critical interpretation or analysis. For example, a health or science writer typically has a degree in biology and can interpret new ideas in the field for the average reader.

Screenwriters prepare scripts for motion pictures or television. They select—or are assigned—a subject, conduct research, write and submit a plot outline or story, and discuss possible revisions with the producer and/or director. Screenwriters may adapt books or plays for film and television. They often collaborate with other screenwriters and may specialize in a particular type of script.

Playwrights write for the stage. They create dialogue and describe action for comedies and dramas. Themes are sometimes adapted from fictional, historical, or narrative sources. Playwrights combine action, conflict, purpose, and resolution to tell stories of real or imaginary life. They often make revisions even while the play is in rehearsal.

Continuity writers prepare material for radio and television announcers to introduce or connect various parts of their programs.

Novelists and *short-story writers* create stories for books, magazines, or literary journals. They use incidents from their own lives, from news events, or from their imagination to create characters, settings, and actions. *Poets* create narrative, dramatic, or lyric poetry for books, magazines, or other publications, as well as for special events such as commemorations.

Requirements

High School   High-school courses that are helpful for a writer include English, literature, foreign languages, general science, social studies, computer science, and typing. The ability to type and familiarity with computers are almost requisites for positions in communications.

Postsecondary   Competition for work as a writer almost always demands the background of a college education.

Many employers prefer people who have a broad liberal arts background or a major in English, literature, history, philosophy, or one of the social sciences. Some employers prefer communications or journalism training in college. Occasionally a master's degree in a specialized writing field may be required. A number of colleges and schools offer courses in journalism, and some of them offer courses in book publishing, publication management, and newspaper and magazine writing.

In addition to formal education, most employers look for practical writing experience. If you have worked on high-school or college newspapers, yearbooks, or literary magazines, you will make a better candidate. Work for small community newspapers or radio stations, even in an unpaid position, is also an advantage. Many book publishers, magazines, newspapers, and radio and television stations have summer internship programs. These provide valuable training if you want to learn about the publishing and broadcasting businesses. Interns do many simple tasks, such as running errands and answering phones, but some may be asked to perform research, conduct interviews, or even write some minor pieces.

Writers who specialize in technical fields may need degrees, concentrated course work, or experience in their subject areas. This usually applies to engineering, business, and the sciences. Also, a degree in technical communications is now offered at many colleges.

If you want a position with the federal government, you will be required to take a civil service examination and meet specific requirements, according to the type and level of the position.

Other Requirements Writers should be creative and able to express ideas clearly, have broad general knowledge, be skilled in research techniques, and be computer-literate. Other assets include curiosity, persistence, initiative, resourcefulness, and an accurate memory. For some jobs—on a newspaper, for example, where the activity is hectic and the deadlines are short—the ability to concentrate and produce under pressure is essential.

Exploring

As a high-school or college student, you can test your interest and aptitude in the field by working as a reporter or writer on school newspapers, yearbooks, and literary magazines. Various writing courses, workshops, and books help you to sharpen your writing skills.

Small community newspapers and local radio stations often welcome contributions from outside sources, although they may not have the resources to pay for them. Jobs in bookstores, magazine shops, and even newsstands can help you become familiar with the various publications.

Information on writing as a career may also be obtained by visiting local newspapers, publishers, or radio and television stations. You may interview some of the writers who work there. Career conferences and other guidance programs often have speakers on the field of communications from local or national organizations.

Employers

Nearly one-third of salaried writers and editors work for newspapers, magazines, and book publishers, according to the *Occupational Outlook Handbook*. Many writers work for advertising agencies, in radio and television broadcasting, or in public relations firms. Others work on journals and newsletters published by business and non-profit organizations. Other employers include government agencies and film-production companies.

Starting Out

Experience is required to gain a high-level position in this field. Most writers start out in entry-level jobs. These jobs may be listed with college placement offices, or you may apply directly to publishers or broadcasting companies. Graduates who have previously served internships with these companies often know someone who can give them a personal recommendation.

Employers in the communications field are usually interested in samples of your published writing. These may be assembled in an organized portfolio or scrapbook. Bylined or signed articles are more helpful than those whose source is not identified.

A beginning position as a junior writer usually involves library research, preparation of rough drafts for a report, cataloging, and other related writing tasks. These are generally carried on under the supervision of a senior writer.

Advancement

Most writers start out as editorial or production assistants. Advancement is often more rapid in small companies, where beginners learn by doing a little of everything and may be given writing tasks immediately. In large firms, however, duties are usually more compartmentalized. Assistants in entry-level positions do research, fact-checking, and copyrighting, but it generally takes much longer to advance to writing tasks.

Promotion into a more responsible position may come with the assignment of more important articles and stories, or it may be the result of moving to another company. Employees in this field often move around. An assistant in one publishing house may switch to an executive position in another. Or a writer may advance by switching to a related field: for example, from publishing to teaching, public relations, advertising, radio, or television.

Freelance or self-employed writers may advance by earning larger fees as they widen their experience and establish their reputation.

Work Environment

Working conditions vary for writers. Although the workweek usually runs thirty-five to forty hours, many writers work overtime. A publication that is issued frequently has more deadlines closer together, which creates greater pressures. The work is especially hectic on newspapers and at broadcasting companies, which operate seven days a week. Writers often work nights and weekends to meet deadlines or to cover a late-developing story.

Most writers work independently, but often they must cooperate with artists, photographers, rewriters, and advertising people. These people may have widely differing ideas of how the materials should be prepared and presented.

The work is sometimes difficult, but writers are seldom bored. Each day brings new and interesting problems. The jobs occasionally require travel. The most difficult aspect is the pressure of deadlines. People who are the most content as writers enjoy and work well under deadline pressure.

Earnings

In 1998, median annual earning for writers were $36,480 a year, according to the *Occupational Outlook Handbook.* Salaries range from $20,920 to $76,660.

In addition to their salaries, many writers earn some income from freelance work. Part-time freelancers may earn from $5,000 to $15,000 a year. Freelance earnings vary widely. Full-time established freelance writers may earn up to $75,000 a year.

Outlook

Employment in this field is expected to increase faster than the average rate of all occupations through 2008. The demand for writers by newspapers, periodicals, book publishers, and nonprofit organizations is expected to increase.

The major book and magazine publishers, broadcasting companies, advertising agencies, public relations firms, and the federal government account for the large number of writers in cities such as New York, Chicago, Los Angeles, Boston, Philadelphia, San Francisco, and Washington, D.C. Opportunities in small newspapers, corporations, and professional, religious, business, technical, and trade publications can be found throughout the United States.

TO LEARN MORE ABOUT WRITERS

Books

Fletcher, Ralph B. *A Writer's Notebook: Unlocking the Writer within You.* New York: Camelot, 1996.

Janeczko, Paul B. *How to Write Poetry.* New York: Scholastic, 1999.

Krull, Kathleen. *Lives of the Writers: Tragedies, Comedies.* Austin: Raintree/Steck-Vaughn, 1998.

New Moon Books Girls Editorial Board. *Writing: How to Express Yourself with Passion and Practice.* New York: Crown, 2000.

Reeves, Diane Lindsey. *Career Ideas for Kids Who Like Writing.* New York: Facts On File, 1998.

Stevens, Carla. *A Book of Your Own: Keeping a Diary or Journal.* New York: Clarion, 1993.

Websites
Creative Writing for Teens
http://teenwriting.about.com
Tips, news, activities, a chat room, and a selection of young authors' works

4Writers
http://www.4writers.com
Support for professional and aspiring writers, plus information about conferences, artists' colonies, and the top creative writing programs

Where to Write
PEN American Center
568 Broadway
New York, NY 10012-3225
Helps foster writers of literary works and provides awards, grants, and support

Writers Guild of America
7000 West Third Street
Los Angeles, CA 90048
For information about this organization that represents writers of all kinds

TO LEARN MORE ABOUT LAURA INGALLS WILDER

Books

Anderson, William. *Laura Ingalls Wilder: A Biography.* New York: HarperCollins, 1992.

Stine, Megan. *The Story of Laura Ingalls Wilder: Pioneer Girl.* Milwaukee: Gareth Stevens, 1996.

Wadsworth, Ginger. *Laura Ingalls Wilder: Storyteller of the Prairie.* Minneapolis: Lerner, 1997.

Websites

Laura Ingalls Wilder: Frontier Girl
http://webpages.marshall.edu/~irby1/laura/frames.html
For a biography of Wilder along with information about her homes and books; includes a children's page

Laura Ingalls Wilder Historic Home and Museum
http://www.bestoftheozarks.com/wilderhome/
For information about Wilder's life and the home in which she wrote the Little House series

The Laura Ingalls Wilder Award
http://www.ala.org/alsc/wilder.html
For information about this honor given by the Association for Library Service to Children, a division of the American Library Association

Where to Write
Laura Ingalls Wilder Memorial Society
105 Olivet Street
De Smet, South Dakota 57231
800/880-3383, Ext. 2

Interesting Places to Visit
Laura Ingalls Wilder Historic Home and Museum
3068 Highway A
Mansfield, MO 65704
417/924-3626

The Laura Ingalls Wilder Memorial Society
105 Olivet Street
De Smet, South Dakota 57231
800/880-3383, Ext. 2

INDEX

Page numbers in *italics* indicate illustrations.

ABOUT THE
AUTHOR

Lucia Raatma received her bachelor's degree in English literature from the University of South Carolina and her master's degree in cinema studies from New York University. Both degrees taught her the power of stories, and very often she feels that the best stories are true ones. She found Laura Ingalls Wilder's life to be one of courage, determination, and pioneering spirit.

Lucia Raatma has written a wide range of books for children and young adults. They include *Libraries* and *How Books Are Made* (Children's Press); an eight-book general-safety series and a four-book fire-safety series (Bridgestone Books); fourteen titles in a character education series (Bridgestone Books); and several titles for Compass Point Books. She has also written career biographies of Maya Angelou, Bill Gates, Charles Lindbergh, and Oprah Winfrey for this series.

When she is not researching or writing, she enjoys going to movies and yoga classes, playing tennis, and spending time with her husband, daughter, and golden retriever. She lives on the west coast of Florida.